# Animal Feeding Time

**FIRST EDITION**
**Project Editor** Deborah Murrell; **Art Editor** Catherine Goldsmith; **Senior Art Editor** Clare Shedden;
**Managing Editor** Bridget Gibbs; **US Editor** Regina Kahney; **Senior DTP Designer** Bridget Roseberry;
**Production** Shivani Pandey; **Picture Librarian** Diane Legrande; **Picture Researcher** Marie Osborn;
**Jacket Designer** Karen Burgess; **Natural History Consultant** Theresa Greenaway;
**Reading Consultant** Linda Gambrell, PhD

**THIS EDITION**
**Editorial Management** by Oriel Square
**Produced for DK** by WonderLab Group LLC
Jennifer Emmett, Erica Green, Kate Hale, *Founders*

**Editors** Grace Hill Smith, Libby Romero, Michaela Weglinski;
**Photography Editors** Kelley Miller, Annette Kiesow, Nicole DiMella;
**Managing Editor** Rachel Houghton; **Designers** Project Design Company;
**Researcher** Michelle Harris; **Copy Editor** Lori Merritt; **Indexer** Connie Binder;
**Proofreader** Larry Shea; **Reading Specialist** Dr. Jennifer Albro; **Curriculum Specialist** Elaine Larson

Published in the United States by DK Publishing
1745 Broadway, 20th Floor, New York, NY 10019

Copyright © 2023 Dorling Kindersley Limited
DK, a Division of Penguin Random House LLC
23 24 25 26 27  10 9 8 7 6 5 4 3 2 1
001–333431–Apr/2023

All rights reserved.
Without limiting the rights under the copyright reserved
above, no part of this publication may be reproduced, stored
in or introduced into a retrieval system, or transmitted, in any
form, or by any means (electronic, mechanical, photocopying,
recording, or otherwise), without the prior written permission
of the copyright owner.
Published in Great Britain by Dorling Kindersley Limited

A catalog record for this book
is available from the Library of Congress.
HC ISBN: 978-0-7440-6693-7
PB ISBN: 978-0-7440-6694-4

DK books are available at special discounts when purchased
in bulk for sales promotions, premiums, fundraising, or
educational use. For details, contact: DK Publishing Special Markets,
1745 Broadway, 20th Floor, New York, NY 10019
SpecialSales@dk.com

Printed and bound in China

The publisher would like to thank the following for their kind permission to reproduce their images:
a=above; c=center; b=below; l=left; r=right; t=top; b/g=background
**Getty Images:** Grant Thomas / iStock 8-9; Moment / Moelyn Photos 28-29; **Dreamstime.com:** Jezbennett 14-15;
**Shutterstock.com:** Binturong-tonoscarpe 32br, diegooscar01 25t, Daniel Guertin 4-5, Katesalin Heinio 34,
Rudi Hulshof 21cr, 30bl, marseus 3, Nicola_K_photos 6-7, Marcin Osman 12-13, Stu Porter 26-27, Dr Morley Read 22-23bc,
30clb (termites), Simply Photos 19, Silvia Truessel 10-11, Oleksandr Umanskyi 16-17
Cover images: *Front:* **123RF.com:** Duncan Noakes l; **Dreamstime.com:** Anastasiya Aheyeva b, Colorfuelstudio crb;
*Back:* **Alamy Stock Photo:** Elvele Images Ltd cla; **Dreamstime.com:** Dragoneye cra, Roomyana ca

All other images © Dorling Kindersley

**For the curious**
**www.dk.com**

Level 1

# Animal Feeding Time

Lee Davis

DK

## Contents

**6**   Morning Meal
**16**  Late Lunch
**26**  Evening Snack

**30** Glossary
**31** Index
**32** Quiz

## Morning Meal

It is morning.
The sun is rising.
Animals that eat
in the daytime
start to look for food.

A gorilla yawns in his nest.
He reaches out his
hairy hand to feel
for a tasty plant.
He has breakfast in bed.

A herd of elephants is ready for breakfast, too. The elephants wrap their trunks around clumps of grass.

They curl their trunks to break off the grass and put it in their mouths.

Another elephant snaps off branches from a big tree. He chews the bark on each branch.

bark

A large elephant knows there are some crunchy seedpods in the tall trees.
He stretches his trunk to reach them.

seedpods

## Late Lunch

Zebras reach down to nibble the grass.

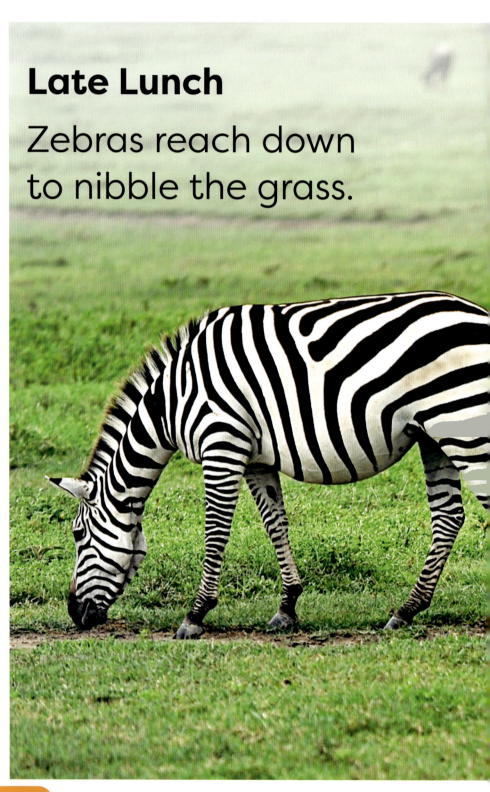

They bite the grass with their front teeth.

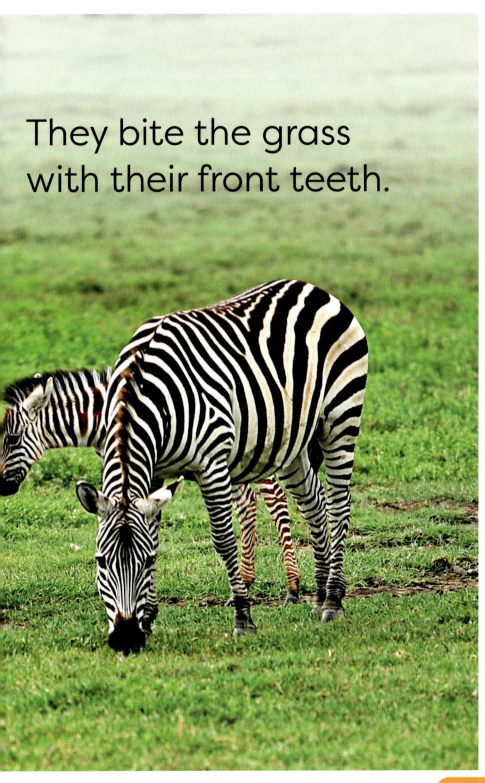

A giraffe can reach
the treetops
with her long neck.
She wraps her tongue
around the tasty,
tender shoots.
Her tongue tears
the shoots
off the branches.

**shoots**

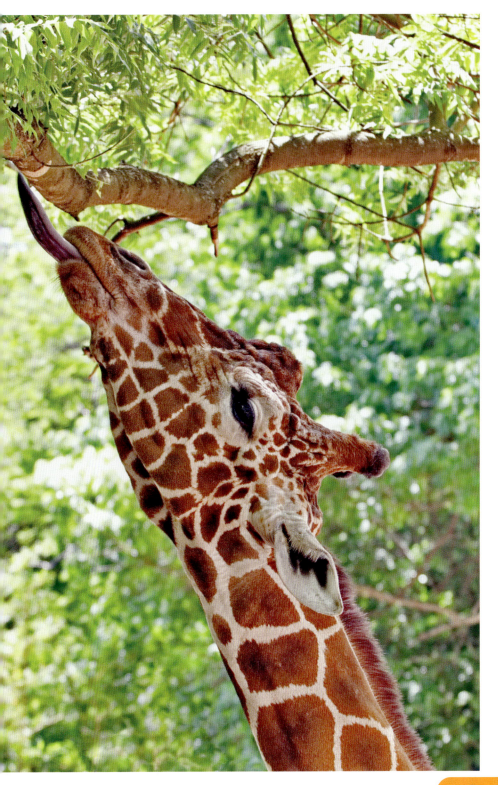

A rhino spends most of the day eating grass. An oxpecker clings to the rhino.

**oxpecker**

The oxpecker eats ticks and insects on the rhino's skin. He pecks at them with his pointed beak.

tick

A chimpanzee is looking for termites to eat.
He digs with a stick into a huge termite hill.
He makes a large hole in the termite hill, and the termites spill out.

termites

A herd of buffalo moves to the river for a drink. Crocodiles watch and wait. They are as still as rocks.

Slowly, a crocodile
swims closer.
Can he grab
a young buffalo
for his dinner?

## Evening Snack

Hippos spend the hot day
in the water.
In the evening,
the air is cooler.

So, they come out to eat the short grass on the river banks.

As the sun sets,
the elephants enjoy
a late evening snack.

They eat more fruit and then have a long, cool drink.

# Glossary

**bark**
the outer part of a tree trunk or branches

**seedpod**
a case with the seeds of a plant inside

**shoot**
young plants that grow from larger ones

**termites**
insects that feed on wood and build mound

**tick**
a bug on the skin of an animal that sucks its blood

# Index

bark  12
branches  12, 18
buffalo  24, 25
chimpanzee  22
crocodiles  24, 25
drink  24, 29
elephants  10, 12, 14, 28
fruit  29
giraffe  18
gorilla  9

grass  10, 11, 16, 17, 20, 27
hippos  26
oxpecker  20, 21
plant  9
rhino  20, 21
seedpods  14
shoots  18
termites  22
ticks  21
zebras  16

# Quiz

Answer the questions to see what you have learned. Check your answers with an adult.

1. What does the gorilla like to eat from its nest?
2. How does the giraffe eat shoots from tree branches?
3. Why does the oxpecker cling to the rhino's back?
4. How does the chimpanzee eat termites?
5. Which animal from this book is your favorite? What does it like to eat?

1. Plants  2. It tears them off the branches with its tongue  3. To eat ticks on the rhino's skin
4. He digs a hole in the termite hill using a stick
5. Answers will vary